#70
Pico Union Branch
1030 S. Alvarado Street
Los Angeles, CA 90006

NOV 2 5 2003

P9-CRO-093

This Is What I Want to Be

Doctor

Heather Miller

1492 99068
x
610
M648

Heinemann Library
Chicago, Illinois

©2003 Reed Educational & Professional Publishing
Published by Heinemann Library,
an imprint of Reed Educational & Professional Publishing
Chicago, IL

Customer Service 888-454-2279
Visit our website at www.heinemannlibrary.com

All rights reserved. No part of this publication may be reproduced or transmitted in any form or by any means, electronic or mechanical, including photocopying, recording, taping, or any information storage and retrieval system, without permission in writing from the publisher.

Designed by Sue Emerson, Heinemann Library
Printed and bound in the United States by Lake Book Manufacturing, Inc.

07 06 05 04 03
10 9 8 7 6 5 4 3 2 1

Library of Congress Cataloging-in-Publication Data
Miller, Heather.
    Doctor / Heather Miller.
        p. cm. — (This is what I want to be)
Includes index.
Summary: Explains the educational background, clothing, equipment, and various duties of a doctor.
    ISBN: 1-4034-0367-8 (HC), 1-4034-0589-1 (Pbk.)
    1. Medicine—Juvenile literature. [1. Physicians. 2. Occupations.] I. Title.
    R130.5.M535 2002
    610.69'52—dc21

2001008134

Acknowledgments
The author and publishers are grateful to the following for permission to reproduce copyright material:

p. 4 Scott Barrow/International Stock; p. 5 Tom & Dee Ann McCarthy/Corbis Stock Market; p. 6 Jim Craigmyle/Masterfile; p. 7 John M. Greim/Mira.com; p. 8 Doug Martin/Photo Researchers, Inc.; p. 9 Joseph Netts/Stock Boston; pp. 10L, 21 David M. Grossman/Photo Researchers, Inc.; p. 10R Blair Seitz/Photo Researchers, Inc.; p. 11 Richard Hutchings/PhotoEdit; p. 12 Andersen Ross/PhotoDisc; p. 13 Jon Feingersh/Corbis Stock Market; p. 14 C. J. Collins/Photo Researchers, Inc.; p. 15 Ed Kashi/Corbis; p. 16 Mike Dobel/Masterfile; p. 17 Bernardo Bucci/Corbis Stock Market; p. 18L EyeWire Collection; p. 18R Will & Deni McIntyre/Photo Researchers, Inc.; p. 19 Gale Zucker/Stock Boston; p. 20 Pictor; p. 23 (row 1, L-R) Richard Hutchings/PhotoEdit, C Squared Studios/PhotoDisc, Corbis; p. 23 (row 2, L-R) Eric Fowke/PhotoEdit, EyeWire Collection, Comstock Images; p. 23 (row 3, L-R) Doug Martin/Photo Researchers, Inc., Jim Craigmyle/Masterfile, Gale Zucker/Stock Boston

Cover photograph by Scott Barrow/International Stock
Photo research by Scott Braut

Every effort has been made to contact copyright holders of any material reproduced in this book. Any omissions will be rectified in subsequent printings if notice is given to the publisher.

Special thanks to our advisory panel for their help in the preparation of this book:

Eileen Day, Preschool Teacher
Chicago, IL

Ellen Dolmetsch, MLS
Wilmington, DE

Kathleen Gilbert,
Second Grade Teacher
Austin, TX

Sandra Gilbert,
Library Media Specialist
Houston, TX

Angela Leeper,
Educational Consultant
North Carolina Department
of Public Instruction
Raleigh, NC

Pam McDonald, Reading Teacher
Winter Springs, FL

Melinda Murphy,
Library Media Specialist
Houston, TX

The publisher would also like to thank Drs. Trina Chapman-Smith and Mark McHaney for their review of this book.

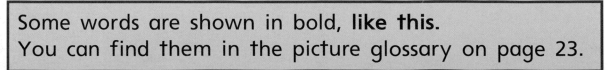

Some words are shown in bold, **like this.**
You can find them in the picture glossary on page 23.

Contents

What Do Doctors Do?

Doctors care for people.

They help people who are sick or hurt.

Doctors teach people.

They help people learn how to
be healthy.

What Is a Doctor's Day Like?

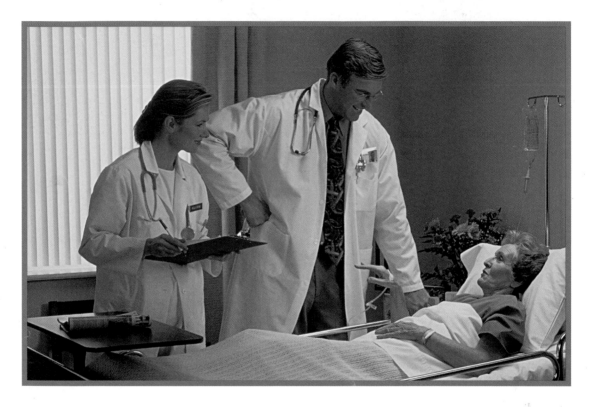

Doctors visit **patients**.

They give **medicine** to people who are sick.

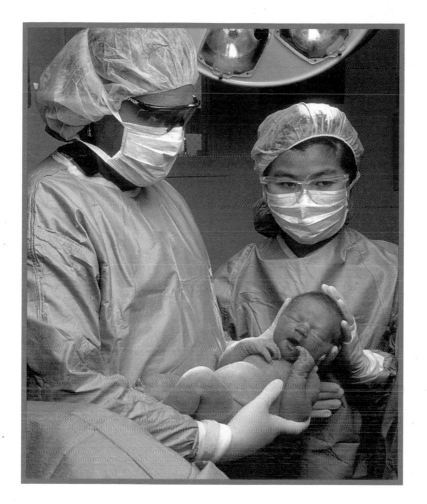

Doctors help when babies are born.

They make sure the babies
are healthy.

What Do Doctors Wear?

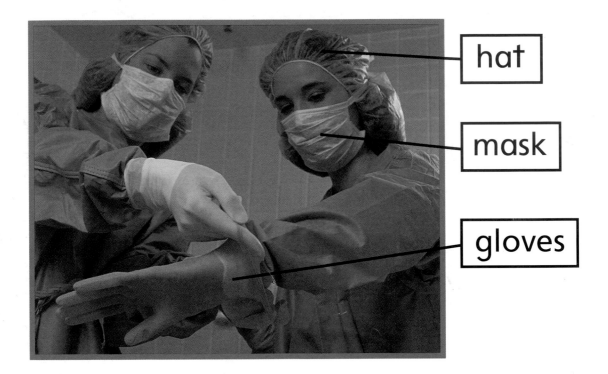

hat

mask

gloves

Sometimes, doctors wear **scrubs.**

Gloves, hats, and **masks** help keep germs away.

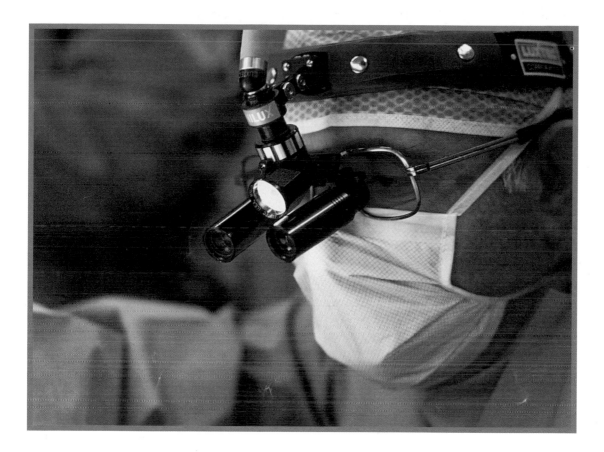

Some doctors wear a light.

It helps them see and work better.

What Tools Do Doctors Use?

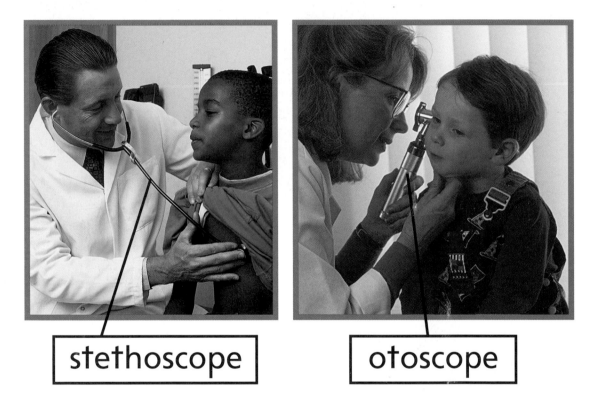

| stethoscope | otoscope |

Doctors listen to your heart with a **stethoscope**.

They look into your ears with an **otoscope**.

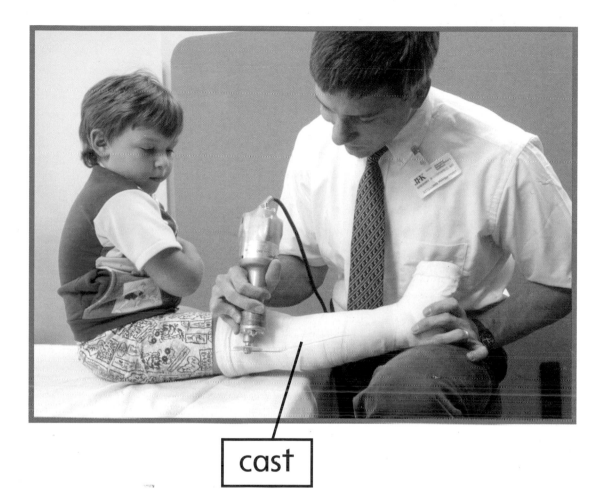

cast

They use a special saw to cut
off **casts**.

Where Do Doctors Work?

Some doctors work in **hospitals**.

Many doctors have their own offices.

Some doctors work in special homes for older people.

Do Doctors Work in Other Places?

Sometimes doctors travel to other countries.

They help people there.

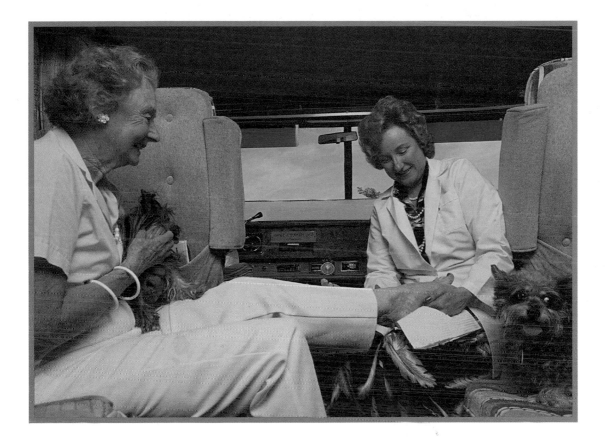

Some doctors drive special vans.

They take care of people in
the van.

When Do Doctors Work?

Doctors work whenever people need them.

They often work at night while other people sleep.

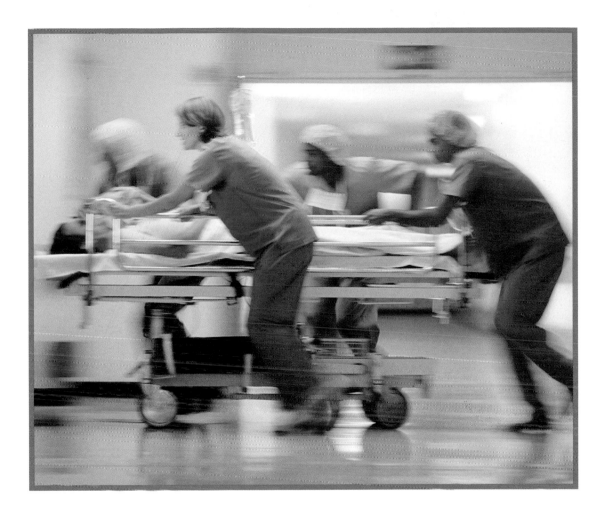

Some people need help right away.

Doctors must always be ready.

What Kinds of Doctors Are There?

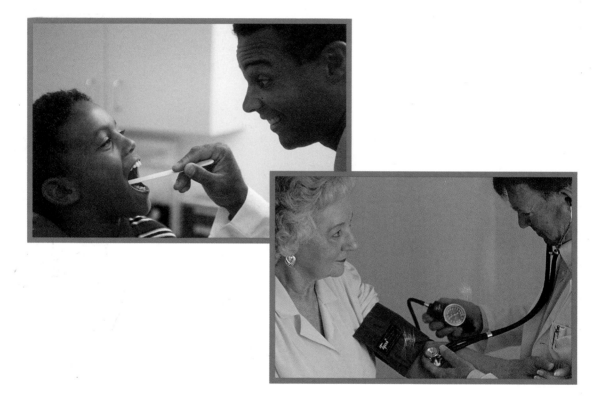

Some doctors work with children.

Other doctors work with older people.

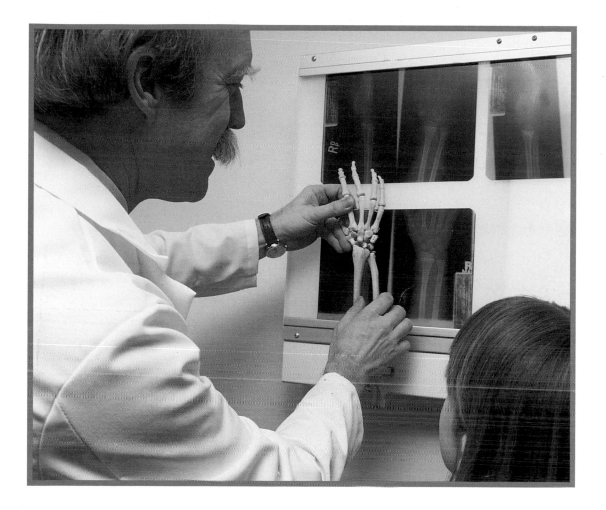

Some doctors look at **X rays**.

Some doctors fix broken bones.

How Do People Become Doctors?

People go to medical school to become doctors.

They learn how the body works.

They work in **hospitals** while they learn.

Can you remember what these things are called?

Look for the answers on page 24.

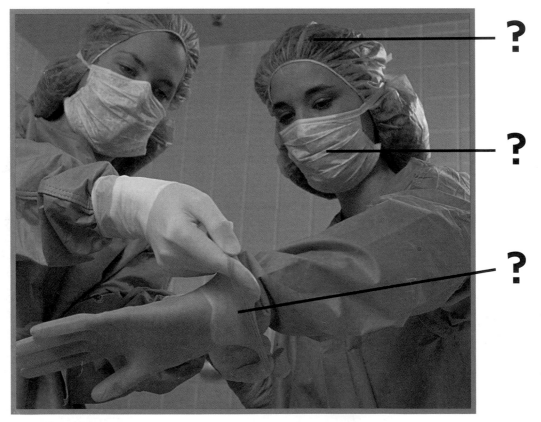

?

?

?

Picture Glossary

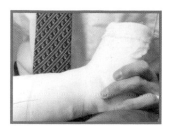

cast
page 11

medicine
page 6

scrubs
page 8

hospital
pages 12, 21

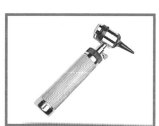

otoscope
page 10

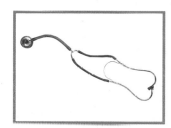

stethoscope
page 10

mask
page 8

patient
page 6

X ray
page 19

Note to Parents and Teachers

Reading for information is an important part of a child's literacy development. Learning begins with a question about something. Help children think of themselves as investigators and researchers by encouraging their questions about the world around them. Each chapter in this book begins with a question. Read the question together. Look at the pictures. Talk about what you think the answer might be. Then read the text to find out if your predictions were correct. Think of other questions you could ask about the topic, and discuss where you might find the answers. Assist children in using the picture glossary and the index to practice new vocabulary and research skills.

Index

Answers to quiz on page 22

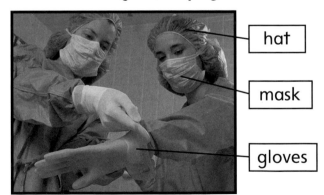

hat

mask

gloves